SPLIT ROCK LIGHTHOUSE

MINNESOTA HISTORIC SITES PAMPHLET SERIES, NO. 15 REVISED

MINNESOTA HISTORICAL SOCIETY PRESS ∽ ST. PAUL

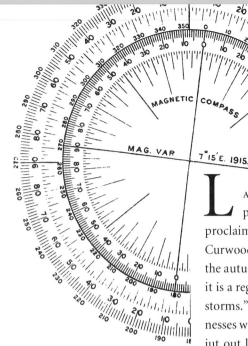

The steamer Lafayette, *1900*

LAKE SUPERIOR is "the most dangerous piece of water in the whole world," proclaimed adventure writer James Oliver Curwood early in 1905. "Here winter falls in the autumn, and from then until late spring it is a region of blizzards and blinding snowstorms." The coasts are "harborless wildernesses with . . . reefs and rocky headlands that jut out like knives to cut ships in two." His words were tragically realized later that year when 116 lives were lost to three violent storms that struck the Great Lakes before the end of the shipping season.

Split Rock Lighthouse owes its existence to the storms of 1905, especially to a record gale on November 28 that damaged nearly 30 ships on Lake Superior alone. The underpowered steel freighters, unable to cope with northeast winds in excess of 60 miles per hour that raged continuously for more than half a day, were driven across the lake toward the rockbound North Shore. "The storm again emphasized the singular peril of lake navigation owing to the proximity of the shore line," concluded a *Marine Journal* editorial the week after the storm. "Had there been searoom probably none of the craft would have been lost. Those that were lost were pounded to pieces on rocks or breakwaters."

Among the shipwrecks was the tow-barge *Madeira*, which broke in two and sank less than a mile northeast of the present lighthouse. The steamer *Lafayette* was demolished on the rocks 12 miles to the southwest, off Encampment Island. Both of these ships were among the extraordinary total of 10 storm-

damaged vessels belonging to the uninsured fleet of the Pittsburgh Steamship Company, a subsidiary of United States Steel Corporation. The *Edenborn* beached without serious damage at the mouth of the Split Rock River, but one of the crew lost his life to the storm. Alarmed by their losses, shipowners petitioned the federal government for aids to navigation along the treacherous shoreline.

Commerce was booming on the Great Lakes during those years. When United States Steel was created by merger in 1901, its fleet of 112 steel freighters became the largest group of American ships belonging to a single owner on any waters. Eastbound shipments of iron ore from Minnesota's giant Mesabi Range escalated at a spectacular rate. From the first order of 2,000 tons in the fall of 1892, shipments of rich hematite from the Duluth-Superior harbor had risen by 1910 to nearly 25 million tons, with traffic from nearby Two Harbors pushing the total beyond 30 million. In the decade and a half before Split Rock Lighthouse was commissioned in 1910, vessels doubled in length and quadrupled in carrying capacity as steam and steel replaced sail

The Lafayette *ashore near Split Rock after the 1905 storm*

and wood. The Sault Ste. Marie canals at the outlet of Lake Superior handled in an eight-month season four times the cargo carried by the Suez Canal.

Behind the statistics was a vision that inspired the promoters of commerce to lofty rhetoric. In a 1908 address entitled "Our Five Inland Seas," Harvey D. Goulder credited "this grand waterway" with such growth in impor-tance to trade and manufacturing that "no man, woman, or child in this country but has felt and enjoyed the beneficent influence and results while people in far off lands have been distinctly benefited." The Cleveland lawyer and general counsel for the Lake Carriers' Association hinted at a kind of divine intention behind it all: "It was the destiny of the United States to be-come the imperial factor in iron and steel and in industrial pursuits. And the destiny of the United States has never yet halted for lack of human instruments."

The shipwrecks of 1905 were an unwelcome interruption to this spiraling success, and Pittsburgh Steamship responded to its losses by launching a campaign for a govern-ment-financed light and fog signal near Split Rock. By the time the Lake Carriers' Association—comprising the owners of more than 500 bulk freight vessels on the lakes—met for its annual meet-ing in January 1907, its most influential mem-ber had been at work behind the scenes. A

> *"November is the archfiend, who in his glowering, dismal thirty days is certain to be harboring with his own horrid mockery a northeast gale."*
>
> —MARY ELLEN CHASE

Ore docks at Two Harbors, 1912

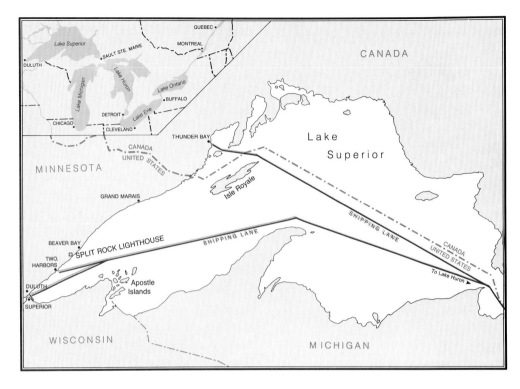

Split Rock Lighthouse and shipping lanes to Sault Ste. Marie

"Some of the Leading Figures at the Annual Convention of the Lake Carriers' Association," as shown in The Marine Review *magazine, February 1910*

petition signed by 85 Great Lakes ship captains demanding a light and fog signal in the vicinity of Split Rock received the convention's unanimous approval.

"It is extremely difficult to locate Two Harbors in a fog or storm prevalent on Lake Superior," asserted the Lake Carriers' Association statement, which went on to list several of the hazards—"the uncertain variation of the compass along the north shore of Lake Superior due to the vast metallic deposits in that vicinity," "the fact that there are no soundings until visible shore is reached," and, finally, "the dangerous character of the coast all along the north shore." The Lake Carriers' Association summarized its case for a federal appropriation in the following words: "During the last three years considerably over one million dollars' worth of vessels and cargoes have been wrecked in the vicinity of Split Rock Point. [The petitioners] believe that a lighthouse and fog whistle established near that point will do away with the serious danger to lives and property, which our experience has shown is due to the fact that there is no warning light or signal."

At the same time, the Lighthouse Board

in Washington, D.C., was receiving a report from its 11th District office that generally agreed with the petitioners but that put the arguments advanced by the shipmasters in a different perspective. The reporting officers dismissed out of hand the necessity of a light alone at this point. "It is not . . . obvious what service a light at Split Rock can perform, since during clear weather neither light nor fog signal at that place is needed for the short run of 45 miles from Devils Island to Two Harbors, and during thick weather, no light is of any service."

The critical issue then became the value of a fog signal. The district office shifted the final burden of cause from the perilous coastal geography back upon the sharp business practices of the vessel owners themselves: "It is a well known fact that vessels in the iron ore trade make a practice of running under virtually full speed, regardless of fog or thick weather. But for this feature of present practice, there would be no need of either a light or fog signal at or near Split Rock Point, since the light at Two Harbors serves as a coast light and guide to that harbor during ordinary weather, and the fog signal at that place is amply sufficient for the guidance of vessels overtaken by fog when near that harbor."

The report went on to note that the unusual magnetic properties of mineral deposits on shore tended to deflect the compass needle eastward and thus direct the ship toward the shore above its Two Harbors destination, where the great depth of the water prevented shipboard soundings until the vessel was dangerously close to shore. Thus, a fog signal at Split Rock might prevent shipwrecks. "Of greater importance than the number of wrecks is, however, the fact that in the ab-

"Porphyry and Greenstone, the latter much disturbs the Compass Needle. The depth of Water everywhere too great for a Vessel to Anchor."

—LT. HENRY W. BAYFIELD'S
CHART OF THE NORTH SHORE,
1825

sence of a fog signal at Split Rock, vessels are greatly delayed in making Two Harbors, and, because of the large number of vessels involved, the money loss due to this delay must be very considerable." Such thoughts could not have been far from the minds of the shipowners at that very moment. A full complement of Lake Carriers' Association members, including Harvey Goulder and Harry Coulby, the president of Pittsburgh Steamship, had already descended upon Washington, D.C., with a grocery list of navigational aids in hand. A lighthouse at Split Rock topped their list.

On January 8 Congressman Theodore E. Burton from Cleveland, Ohio—characterized by association president William Livingstone as a "true, honest and hard-working friend of the Lake Carriers' association and one who has displayed great knowledge, intelligence and energy in dealing with lake improvements"— introduced a bill for a light and fog signal in the vicinity of Split Rock. Senator Knute Nelson of Minnesota followed suit in the Senate. In open congressional hearings shortly after their arrival, both Coulby and Goulder lobbied strongly for the measure, the latter characterizing the need for increased navigational aids on Lake Superior as being similar to "a boy growing out of his clothes."

His rhetoric was not lost on the committeemen. The bill passed routinely through the 59th Congress, and in March 1907, $75,000 was approved for lighthouse and fog signal construction at Split Rock as part of an overall appropriation that befitted the expansionist spirit of the times—a half-million dollars to be spent for new lighthouses on the Great Lakes alone.

BUILDING THE LIGHT

∾

"GOOD FOR A LIGHTHOUSE," wrote surveyor Thomas Clark in his journal while mapping the rugged coastline between Duluth and Beaver Bay in 1854. A month before Clark's visit, the signing of a treaty with the Ojibway had opened up the North Shore to non-Indian settlement. In the summer of 1856 the Reverend James Peet, an early missionary at the head of the lakes, took refuge in a nearby cove ("3" on Clark's sketch—later called Little Two Harbors) when a northeast squall made the water too rough for his tiny sailboat. He was returning to Superior from Beaver Bay, a settlement scarcely seven weeks old.

When the engineers of the Lighthouse Board selected the site for the new station half a century later they agreed with Clark's judgment about the rocky promontory, which was known locally as Stony Point. Although "Split Rock" is the name by which the lighthouse became known, the origin of the term is shrouded in speculation. Canadian officer Henry W. Bayfield, who surveyed the lake in 1825, used the name to refer to the river located two and a half miles southwest of the lighthouse. It remains unclear whether the name derived from the geological fact of the river splitting the rock canyon through which it passes or simply from the appearance of the rock itself—the white streaks of anorthosite running through the black igneous diabase seem, in fact, to "split the rock." Other theorists derive the name from cliffs northeast of the river, one or both of which have been variously known as Split Rock Point because, when viewed from the water, they look like one rock that is split apart.

In any event, the name came to be applied to the lighthouse when the shipowners who lobbied in Washington for the establishment of a light in the region proposed that it be

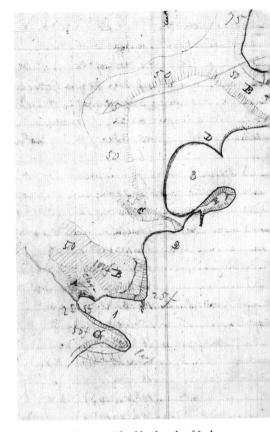

Surveyor Thomas Clark's sketch of Lake Superior's coastline, 1854, with the Split Rock promontory at letter "E"

built "in the vicinity of Split Rock, Minnesota, preferably on Corundum Point." Because it was erroneously believed that valuable abrasive minerals existed at the latter, the site chosen for the light station was on Stony Point, farther to the northeast. The name Split Rock stuck, however, and came to be applied to the entire region between the lighthouse and the river.

When construction boats arrived in May 1909, the first job was to find a way to raise the building materials to the top of the cliff. "The initial undertaking was to land and install a powerful hoisting engine," recalled engineer Ralph Russell Tinkham. "This was landed from a barge on the rocky shore of the small cove at the south end of the cliff where a rough steep slope extends from the shore line up behind the cliff to its summit." The men cut a swath through the dense woods, and although the vital steam engine and

The youthful lighthouse architect-engineer, Ralph Russell Tinkham

boiler tipped over halfway up the slope, it eventually reached the top. "Mounted on skids this hoisting engine was made to pull itself up the steep slope with lines and tackle attached to trees on the slope above it," wrote Tinkham.

Once the hoisting engine was in place, "installed and housed near the cliff edge north of the corundum outcrop," Tinkham continued, the workers devised a method for hauling all their supplies up to the lighthouse site. "Using an improvised A-frame and tackle at the edge of the vertical cliff," the men hoisted "the components of a heavy duty stiff legged derrick . . . from a barge moored to ring bolts anchored in the rock cliff at lake level, a hundred feet below the ground level of the station site. This derrick was then erected near the top edge of the cliff, securely anchored to the rock surface, and thereafter

A crude hoist lifting construction materials from a cruiser, 1909

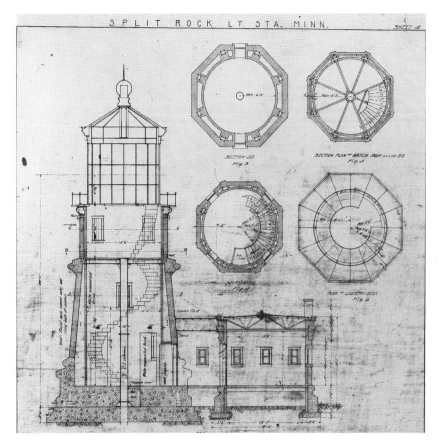

Tinkham's original section drawing of the Split Rock light tower

was used throughout the construction of the station for hoisting all materials, equipment, and supplies from the barges, or the cruiser, including the lifting or lowering of personnel in a box crate, called a skip."

After the site and a large area around it had been cleared of brush and trees, the workers began at once to drill and dynamite for the building foundations. At the same time they erected the three wooden storage barns and used them as temporary living quarters while building the three brick keepers' homes. Life at the construction site had its hazards. Tinkham, who occupied the second floor of the first barn, later recalled: "One memorable evening I stood in my quarters watching the blasting preparations through the window. When the blast went off, one of the logs covering the blast area, a log of ten inches in diameter and eight feet long, rose into the air and sailed end first through a high trajectory over the warehouse and down through the open flap entrance of one of the

*The completed keepers'
houses with the girders of the
unfinished light tower, 1909*

long tents, landing with a crash on the floor between the bunks. Men came scrambling out of the rear end of the tent like ants. Immediately after this eruption rock fragments of all sizes, up to that of a football, were scattered far and wide. I saw one the size of my head coming in my direction, and as I ducked away from the window, it struck the roof above my quarters and rolled rumbling to the ground. Curiously, no one ever was injured by these occasional bombardments."

When the foundations were done, successive waves of carpenters, concrete workers, steelworkers, and bricklayers proceeded to the remote site. By November 1909, when the workers stopped for the winter, the steel girders of the tower were rooted in the rock outcropping. The last workers escaped the site by hiking through the woods to catch a logging train down the shore to Duluth, where Tinkham led them, rifles and knapsacks in hand, into the fashionable Spalding

Hotel for a drink. Work resumed the next spring, and the station stood complete and ready for occupancy in midsummer of 1910.

Many of the construction workers were immigrants, like Peter Sundstrom, who was typical of the young Scandinavians who settled the region early in the 20th century. Entering Boston in 1906 with $20 and the address of a former neighbor in hand, he and three fellow Swedes traveled to Wheaton, Minnesota, where they worked for 15 cents an hour. The following year the 20-year-old man and his companions signed on with an itinerant construction outfit, L. D. Campbell Company of Duluth. During the next two years they helped build a railroad trestle in Montana, a tannery in Red Wing, and the city hall in Hibbing. When Campbell bid successfully on the Split Rock job in early 1909, Sundstrom arrived at the construction site with the first boatload of workers, including a French cook and his family.

Except for an occasional escape to Two Harbors on the *Red Wing* or to Duluth on board the passing *America,* men like Sundstrom worked long days at 35 cents an hour. Living in tents, they endured one storm so severe that all the men had to stay in the main tent and hold it down to keep it from blowing away. They rode the precarious skip down to unload the supply scow; they rained endless sledgehammer blows on the hand drills that the three-man teams rotated while preparing the rock for dynamiting. Sundstrom himself, with his growing carpentry skills, used and reused the wooden forms that painstakingly built up the concrete foundation for the rugged tower. Like the ensuing gangs of ironworkers and bricklayers, he left the camp when his own task was completed, never to see the light in operation. Between the 1909 and 1910 construction seasons at Split Rock, Sundstrom worked for Campbell on a hotel in Brule, Wisconsin. The following spring the hotel's foundation thawed and then collapsed, and soon afterwards the firm went bankrupt. Split Rock light station was to be its last successful job.

KEEPING THE LIGHT

"ONE OF THE GREAT DISADVANTAGES upon the obtainment of good keepers," lamented a government lighthouse survey in the late 19th century, "is the rate of salary allowed, which, in this country will not command the services of intelligent men, such as are required to do justice to a valuable and costly apparatus, when such is entrusted to them." Fortunately, this was never the case at Split Rock. Although the turnover of new and unskilled

The lower section of the tramway, completed in 1916 to replace the derrick at the top of the cliff

SCALING THE CLIFF: THE SPLIT ROCK TRAMWAY

DURING the light's first years of operation, the hazardous construction derrick was the only way to bring supplies up to the station from the lakeshore. Using funds left over from the original appropriation, the Lighthouse Service decided to build a tramway to improve the station's access to the water. In the fall of 1915 lighthouse tenders deposited materials to begin construction on the upper leg of the tramway. Working until the opening of the deer-hunting season, local laborers laid the track from the oil house as far down as the new brick tram house. By the following summer they had completed the lower portion to the lake.

The renovated tramcar from the original derrick was able to raise a three-ton load up the steep slope to the turntable next to the tram house, where the load was detached from the cable and pushed by hand up the rails to the dwelling complex. In 1929 the first modern road was built into the light station from the newly completed North Shore highway. The tramway was eventually dismantled in 1934 when the station received a truck to haul its supplies in by road.

Visitors climb to the restored lighthouse and the fog station building (at left) that houses air compressors.

men as second assistants remained a chronic problem, the first assistants were seasoned veterans, and the keepers themselves, by any standard, were resourceful men devoted to their calling and capable of exceptional, even heroic service. All this despite meager wages that forced these same men to labor at painting, paperhanging, and other odd wintertime careers to support their families.

Orren ("Pete") Young began his lighthouse career in 1901, earning $425 a year. After serving at several lighthouses along Lake Superior's Michigan coast as a second and first assistant, he received $624 a year as the initial keeper of Split Rock Lighthouse in 1910. When he retired in 1928 at the age of 70, he was earning $1,500 a year. Franklin J. Covell began his career at Split Rock in 1913 as a second assistant earning $456 a year. After tours of duty at several stations around the head of the lakes, including lighthouses at Superior and Two Harbors, he returned twice to Split Rock, the second time to stay in 1924. He was promoted from first assistant to succeed Young in 1928 at a salary of $1,380 a year. During the depression his pay remained fixed, and when he retired at the mandatory age of 70 in late 1944, he was earning $1,680 a year.

The keeper and his two assistants were of necessity jacks-of-all-trades. A tradition in the lighthouse service held that the best keepers were old sailors, and indeed Pete Young had sailed aboard the lumber hookers from Michigan to Buffalo in his youth. But it was more a knowledge of weather, the sea, and nature's subtle caprices than a knack for handling boats that made men like Keeper

Split Rock Lighthouse, isolated above the nation's largest inland sea

Keeper Pete Young in the doorway of the fog station building, 1926

Young and later Keeper Covell such consummate caretakers of their light. Skill and experienced judgment played an important part in knowing when to operate equipment like the fog signal, as well as in keeping both the horn and the light functioning at a constant rate.

Through the night the keeper and assistants rotated four-hour watches, and during the day they kept a weather eye out as part of their normal eight-hour workday around the station. If the foghorn was sounding, as it did at 20-second intervals when visibility dropped below five or so miles, the men stood the daytime watch in the fog signal building.

It was not unusual over the years to find the station short a man for periods that sometimes stretched to weeks or even months. The watches then became more demanding, alternating every six hours, and other duties piled up accordingly.

Because the lighthouse was far from the service's supply depots in Detroit and Duluth, the early keepers had to be skilled at repairing as well as operating the equipment, often without the luxury of suitable parts or tools.

Despite the presence of backup air compressors for the fog signal machinery, maintenance problems with the original gasoline engines called for much ingenuity on top of backbreaking labor. This resourcefulness was needed to keep other services vital to the station operating as well. Besides dealing with recurrent problems involving plumbing, heating, and water supply, the men were pressed into service as carpenters, cement workers, road builders, and gardeners. Keeper Young even cooked and kept house for the laborers hired to construct the steep tramway in 1915.

"Don't look down—it'll make you dizzy!" was Keeper Covell's simple prescription for scrambling atop the steel lighthouse lantern to paint the black ventilator ball 184 feet above the water. Storm damage to the docks, boats, and outbuildings had to be attended to as well as the regular repairs around the tower, fog signal, tramway, and dwellings. Annual painting chores included every varnished and painted surface inside and the bright red metal roofs atop the dwellings. Other demanding seasonal duties involved handling bulk supplies of coal, gasoline, and kerosene; cutting endless cords of wood for the kitchen stoves

> *"To run a station Dad had to be a painter, a carpenter, a machinist, fireman, engineer, first-aider, housekeeper. . . ."*
>
> —CLARENCE H. YOUNG

Fisherman George Hanson of Little Two Harbors, about 1915

NEXT-DOOR NEIGHBORS

ACROSS THE COVE to the west of the lighthouse a small fishing village grew up in the period before World War I. Known as "Little Two Harbors" because of the island that divided the bay into two coves, the tiny community had a dock for commercial fishing boats like the *Grace J,* which stopped to pick up barrels of salted fish and sell needed supplies to keepers and fishermen alike. Four or five Norwegian fishermen lived in the village, the only residents to remain through the harsh winters. Some of them became hunting and drinking companions of the early assistant keepers and helped to build the elevated tramway at the lighthouse. One of the immigrants was eventually drafted for war service, and by 1925 the last occupant had sold the land and returned to his homeland.

Early Tragedy at Split Rock: Two Assistants Lost at Sea

SCARCELY TWO MONTHS after the lighthouse was commissioned in 1910, Keeper Young sent his two assistants to Beaver Bay for the mail. His son Clarence recalled: "Dad (being an old sailor [who] could sail anything that would float) rigged a sail for the little boat with a mast and a rudder. He would just hold the end of the sail in his hand, so if a sudden gust of wind came, he could let it go. One day he caught one of them with the sail tied to the seat and told them to never, never tie the sail down, as a quick puff of wind would tip the boat over. One day they went out and didn't come back. The boat was found on the beach upside down with the sail still tied to the seat. The men were never found."

Assistant Keeper Harry Thompson's journal for 1916 includes mention of a tenth wedding anniversary spent tending the fog signal, an inspection, and receipt of a keg of beer.

and furnaces; hauling water for the dwellings; and even transporting loads of dirt fill—once brush and stumps had been removed—to turn the exposed rock face into landscapes where trees and gardens might be planted. Everything from polishing the lens and washing windows to converting the barns into garages and building a road from the boathouse to the dwellings was accepted as normal duty for a lighthouse keeper at Split Rock.

On top of this, the keeper functioned as an administrator, bookkeeper, and bureaucrat. He had to handle the men in his charge and cope with problems of incompetence and alcoholism. He had to keep detailed records of everything from the number of hours the fog signal operated to the contents of the station medicine chest. Finally, he had to carry on an unending and often frustrating correspondence with his superiors in Detroit in order to obtain a needed part or inaugurate the slightest change in established procedure.

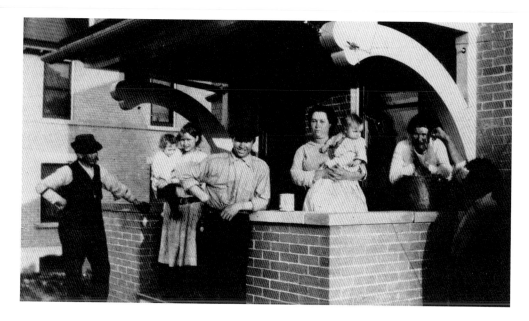

Keeper Young (left) with Assistant Keeper Franklin D. Covell's family and Assistant Keeper Harry Thompson (right), about 1915

Assistant keepers Lee Benton and Gilbert Hanson with young Harold Benton, 1910

He himself needed formal permission to leave the lighthouse station for longer than six hours at a time.

The early keepers had diverse skills that enriched their personal lives as well as contributed to their survival in harsh surroundings. Keeper Young made most of his household furnishings by hand and on occasion gave his first assistant a haircut. Keeper Covell played the violin and grew ginseng root as well as potatoes in his garden. Both men hunted, fished, and trapped. Later on Keeper Covell would add to his many hats that of truck mechanic and even tour guide as the light attracted visitors in growing numbers. Split Rock was indeed exceptional in having able, unstinting leadership through its years of operation.

ALL IN A DAY'S WATCH

A POWERFUL FOG SIGNAL was not always enough to ward off disaster along the dangerous coastline, since sound traveled in capricious ways that could deceive even the most experienced mariners. In 1912 the old lumber steamer *Viking* went on the rocks in the fog while the horns at Split Rock were sounding two miles away. A happier incident in the summer of 1930 demonstrated that people will perhaps never be replaced by their technological inventions.

Keeper Covell's daughter recalled the day: "My aunt, uncle, and cousin had come to visit from the state of Washington. We were out on the front walk preparing to go down to the car for a trip into town. The road then went to the boathouse. The fog signal was sounding fog, and Dad picked up right away the sounding of this ore boat. He ran to the fog signal, and they put up pressure and sounded the danger signal. The ore boat didn't answer, but just kept sounding fog. Dad started for the boathouse on a run with all the rest of us fast on his trail."

Although the boat was still invisible, its own foghorn indicated it was drawing ever closer to the rocky shallows of the cove west of the light. At the boathouse Keeper Covell located a small tin whistle and rushed to the end of the dock. The fog hung so thick that he could see nothing, yet he could hear voices on board the approaching boat. He blew the danger signal. The boat answered at once. There came the thunderous churning of the propeller reversing itself. The unseen carrier removed once again to safety.

Disaster averted is disaster forgotten. Or, as daughter Ileana remembered: "They got out into the lake, gave a salute, and were on their way." Keeper Covell's own words in the lighthouse log for the day, July 26, 1930, remained typically spartan: "Attending fog signal; heavy fog most of the day; a large boat came nearly running on the island at 11 AM; by the aid of hand horn the Keeper was able to turn them before they struck."

A 55-year-old man's quick thinking had spared a ship so near the rocky cliff that the sound waves from the mechanical foghorn had deflected unheard overhead.

A foggy night at Split Rock

Lee Benton, assistant keeper, with the gasoline air compressors that powered the fog signals, about 1911

The pantry, as it looked about 1920

LIVING AT THE LIGHT
~

WHAT WAS IT LIKE to grow up in the long shadow cast by the lighthouse? Waves pounding the caves beneath the cliff so hard the whole rock quaked. Gale winds driving the spray completely over the promontory, sculpting ice an inch thick on the east windows. Water pipes and ink bottles freezing, hot-water heat failing. Lightning storms knocking down curtains and making the telephone dance in the dining room. Summer nights so idyllically quiet that fish could be heard jumping far below in the dark water. The rhythm of a guitar and gospel singing on the front steps, or through an open window a hand-wound Victrola playing records newly arrived by boat from Chicago. Such were the early contrasts in life at Split Rock.

Although Pete Young served as keeper for 18 seasons, his family never made its home at the lighthouse, choosing to live at Munising, Michigan, at Duluth, and finally at neighboring Two Harbors. As his four children grew older, they made summer visits to their father's residence nearest the tower. Beginning in 1916 they arrived—often alone—on the fashionable passenger steamer *America* to enter a pastoral world where deer ate the lettuce in the garden and the nearest permanent village was a 45-minute boat ride away at tiny Beaver Bay. In addition to washing and cooking for her father, daughter Grace later took charge of the station's first-aid kit and even stood afternoon watch in the living room with a pair of binoculars.

Keeper Frank Covell's wife and three oldest children accompanied him when he first served at Split Rock from 1913 to 1916. When he returned to occupy the middle dwelling in 1924, his two youngest daughters were growing up. In 1931 the family began to live at the station year-round, and the stepchildren of First Assistant Justus G. Luick moved into the first house to become playmates of the younger Covell sisters.

Although the children were strictly forbidden to play around the tower or fog signal, or to tag along with the growing number of tourists visiting the station, they were occasionally permitted to accompany their father on his rounds. Ileana Covell recalled: "I used to go with Dad up into the tower and wind up the cable, while he pumped up the pressure in the tank for the mantle." Luick's stepdaughter, Marilyn Brookins, found the tower a safe fortress—"like a battleship"—except for the rare ventures to the very top of it: "There was a door that opened up to the gangway going around the outside of the light. I was never able to get all the way around. About halfway around, I began to get dizzy and weak, so I would have to turn back, and Mr. Luick helped me and would have to half-carry me back."

The fog signal building stood on firmer ground. Marilyn often joined her stepfather when the horn was sounding: "My stepfather's watch would begin at 8:00 P.M., so I used to take my coloring book, or whatever, and stay there with him until maybe 10:00 P.M. During these times when it was so foggy outside, the inside of the fog signal, warmed by the steam from the cisterns and engines, seemed so cozy. I was totally happy, and used to lie on my stomach on the cistern cover, which was nice and warm.

"Meanwhile Mr. Luick would be doing things like polishing the brass, oiling the engines, or just reading his paper. But it was

> *"I was twelve the first summer the family went to Split Rock from Duluth on the* SS America. *It was really an experience getting off the big boat down into a small skiff tossing around on a one-and-a-half-foot sea, seven or eight feet below us."*
>
> —CLARENCE H. YOUNG

during these times when he would answer never-ending questions of 'What's this?' and 'What's it for?'"

Although the tower and fog signal building remained generally off limits—except for slides down the rear hump of the rock dome in wintertime—the idle tramway became a favorite haunt of the children. On Beulah Covell's return from school to the lighthouse in the mid-1920s, she found the first trip ashore from the rocking *America* frightening, until her father transported her to the top of the rock aboard the tiny tramcar. The tracks themselves were of more interest to Marilyn, who learned to tightrope walk their entire length. Other tricks she performed to shock the tourists (eventually she joined the circus) included riding her brother's bicycle

The America, *returning to Duluth from one of its three weekly runs along the lakeshore, about 1910*

The keepers' children at Split Rock, about 1925, with tram tracks in foreground

Franklin D. Covell in 1914, head keeper from 1928 to 1944

from the light station down to the tram house on the narrow planks laid between the rails. Forced away from the dwellings, where their off-duty fathers slept during the day, the children clambered upon the turntable in front of the hoist house. Sunset often found them lingering there on concrete that was still warm from the heat of the day, singing together and playing noisy guessing games.

Beyond the station itself the whole out-of-doors formed a vast natural playground. Collecting agates on the beach, building wooden boats, picnicking on the island at Little Two Harbors, or picking berries in the nearby hills—all were common pleasures for the sons and daughters of Split Rock. They enjoyed an unusual closeness to the wildlife that abounded in the surrounding woods. "I always went with my father into the woods to help cut wood and haul it in," Ileana recalled. "I knew all the animals about and could tell which ones had been around by their tracks. . . . We would walk through the woods, and he would show me on the trees where the bears were clawing high, and that meant deep snow." They put out food for partridges, watched a woodchuck nurse her young, and made pets of chipmunks, an owl, and even for one season an orphaned bear cub. Another summer Keeper Covell built a lily pond in the backyard and stocked it with goldfish that grew to astonishing size.

But nothing could equal the lake trout sunning lazily in the rocky shallows that Keeper Covell's daughters could see from the base of the tower—fish so large that they made the cool, dark caves under the cliff a perfect fishing hole. They made such a startling noise when they jumped that one peaceful evening Keeper Young rushed from the fog signal, worried that his daughter Grace, tarrying by the low wall, had fallen into the lake.

Such evenings were the perfect end to a childhood day at Split Rock. Marilyn Brookins remembered: "In the warm summer evenings we often got together on [the Covells'] front porch with Beulah playing her

A wooden bridge and birch trees along a shoreline hiking trail in the state park

guitar and singing folk songs to us. The lake would be like glass. . . . A glance up the walk, and one would see Mr. and Mrs. Covell walking arm in arm, either on their way to light the light or just coming back from having lit it. All was so peaceful and serene! We could smell the flowers from a little rock garden that Mrs. Covell had on the slope in front of their home. . . . One could take very deep breaths and feel so good."

The children of assistant keepers Hans Christensen and Lee Benton in front of Split Rock's three identical barns and houses, 1911

LIGHTNING STRIKES THE STATION

THE LIGHTNING RODS and sturdy construction of the station's buildings did not forestall dramatic intrusions by the elements. "One of the worst thunderstorms of the season," recorded the lighthouse log for July 20, 1932. "Lightning struck the Keeper's quarters, tower and signal, tearing away a large portion of concrete from the face of tower; storm came from west, fog from northeast." The damage ranged from a prodigious scar on the tower base to hundreds of tiny holes in a lard pail that was placed over the fog signal downspout.

The storm also terrorized the Covell family. As the lightning struck it followed the water pipes into the middle dwelling. Blue and orange flames shot from the faucets into the kitchen sink. The lightning burned through the telephone line as well, setting the candlestick telephone and the Oliver typewriter dancing crazily on the desk in the dining room. Beulah Covell, whose youthful curiosity overcame her mother's order to stay put, poked her head out of the pantry in time to see curtains and rod torn from the window and dumped across the dining room table. "It sounded like each brick in the house was falling," her sister Ileana recalled. "Mother said, 'Let them fall!'" No one was injured, and in a matter of seconds nature's most bizarre assault on the exposed promontory was over.

"I remember that a lightning 'ball' came inside of Mr. Covell's house, raced around the dining room wall, entered the front room, went under the couch or davenport where Mr. Covell kept his violin, and broke the strings on it."

—MARILYN BROOKINS
BLIEVERNICHT

STANDING FOR INSPECTION

❧

EACH YEAR the lighthouse tenders *Amaranth* and *Marigold* visited the light station, anchoring offshore and sending a small launch to the dock west of the light. In the early days they deposited keepers at the isolated station in the spring and sometimes took them away in the winter. Most often, however, these 150-foot steam vessels delivered equipment or vital supplies of coal, gasoline, or kerosene. At least once a season the visits took on an added element of surprise and excitement—an 11th District superintendent would be on board to inspect the station.

The visits of the tenders were never announced and could occur at any hour of the day from sunup to sundown. The keepers, however, learned to anticipate their arrival and even to counter one superintendent's strategy of coming straight across the lake, hiding the ship in the bright sunlight. A pennant on the mast betrayed the inspector's presence on board, and one assistant keeper offered 50 cents to the keen-eyed child who was the first to spot the tiny flag. Nevertheless, the warning was only a matter of minutes, and an inevitable flurry of activity followed to ready the station for official scrutiny.

Each man had his station and last-minute duties to perform to ensure clean floors, spotless equipment, and a proudly flying flag. But perhaps the most onerous duty was getting into uniform. Ordered by mail at the keeper's own expense, the uniforms were too bulky and uncomfortable to be worn other than on Sundays or special occasions, and lower assistants often did not bother to acquire one at all. The keeper himself had little choice in the matter: he must be formally attired—complete with black tie, white shirt, and starched collar and cuffs—and standing on the dock to greet the inspector. If the keeper had been painting or cleaning in the tower, he had to hasten back to his dwelling, where the entire family might be called into service to help him dress and descend the steep hill in time.

In addition to checking vital equipment in the tower and the fog signal building, the inspector was duty-bound to examine the residences, even to poking his head in closets and pantries or into the ovens of the wood-burning stoves, where he might find anything from dirty dishes to freshly baking bread. More than one plate of warm biscuits helped to relax a strict attention to regulations in the dwellings themselves. And on one occasion Keeper Young's daughter Grace gave the superintendent a lesson on how to starch his collars in cold water. The inspector's visit was also the occasion for a general meeting in the fog signal building, sometimes to air grievances or to mediate a minor dispute in the lighthouse community, but more often to consider matters of maintenance and repair. After reviewing the lighthouse log the inspector formally signed the book and

> *"Word always seemed to get to the light that the* Amaranth *was at Devil's Island light. Devil's Island is, I'd say, about southeast as you're standing up by the fog signal, so the first curl of smoke on the horizon would send up a shout."*
>
> —ILEANA COVELL MYERS

The lighthouse tender Amaranth, *awaiting the launch that ferried supplies to Split Rock's dock, about 1915*

pronounced the station fit and in proper working order.

Inspection day was an especially exciting time for the Split Rock children, who hovered around the dock to pass judgment themselves upon these visitors from the outside world. The ship's crew was a friendly lot, and one superintendent gave Grace Young two poetry books from the portable libraries that were exchanged every year at the more remote stations. If the inspector was not on board the tender after all, it might mean a chance to ride out to the vessel and even to have dinner at the captain's table. In a few hours—all too soon from the children's point of view—the visit would be over and the tender on its way to surprise another light station along Lake Superior's shores.

> *"My father hardly had time to dress in his uniform. He'd be buttoning up his shirt while I'd be lacing up his shoes."*
>
> —GRACE YOUNG VOKOVAN

The keeper's house bedroom, restored to pre-electricity era of 1920s

The keeper's house kitchen with wood-burning cookstove

A LESSON IN LIGHTHOUSE TECHNOLOGY

~

ONE MUST FORGET for a moment the world of computers and telecommunications to appreciate the ingenuity of classic lighthouse technology. Although both electricity and the internal combustion engine were in wide use by the beginning of the 20th century, the lighthouse beacons, by virtue of their isolated settings, were generally denied the benefit of such civilized advancements. Yet for all their reliance upon principles of traditional mechanics and preelectrical energy, they had evolved into sophisticated mechanisms capable of great precision. The towers and their lights, like the men who served them, had to be at once ruggedly independent and as dependable as the night was long.

More than a century before the Split Rock light was built, United States lighthouses had begun to revolve their lights—then composed of a variable number of wick-based oil lamps—to produce the regular flashing signals that identified each individual light to passing ships. This rotation was accomplished by a clockwork mechanism essentially like the one installed at Split Rock. A gearbox attached to the base of the lens pedestal was connected to a cable that had to be wound by hand every two hours through the night. This cable supported a column of disk weights that dropped by gravity through the hollow mast at the center of the tower. Their vertical descent was translated into the horizontal rotation of the entire lens assembly.

The next important innovation was the development in 1822 of the annular or ring-shaped lens by French physicist Augustin-Jean Fresnel. The light could now be flashed by rotating only the lens assembly while the light source itself remained stationary at a central focal point. By the 1890s a tray of

mercury began to be used as a bearing surface. With the lens literally floating in 250 pounds of liquid mercury, it became possible to rotate the mammoth, two-and-one-half ton apparatus fast enough so that only two lens panels were necessary to produce a frequent signal. Since fewer individual panels meant less diffusion of light from the central source,

The light's clamshell-style lens, constructed with 242 prisms

a substantial increase in the brightness could be obtained from the same lamp.

Reflecting and refracting prisms recovered 60 percent of the light emitted from the fixed source and concentrated it into two beams that emerged from the central magnifying portion of each lens panel. The characteristic flash that swept the horizon once every 10 seconds at Split Rock was created by adjusting a mechanical governor on the clockwork mechanism so that the entire lens assembly made one complete revolution every 20 seconds.

The latest technological revolution was still in progress in 1910. Scarcely a half-dozen years before, the first incandescent oil vapor lamp had been introduced in the United States. The same Lake Carriers' Association that lobbied successfully for Split Rock Lighthouse soon urged the universal adoption of these new lamps. By the time the lighthouse stood completed, the lamps had become standard equipment and helped make the Split Rock light one of the most powerful of the more than 400 lighthouses and beacons shining on the Great Lakes.

The brass fuel assembly of initially a double and later a single tank fit snugly against the rotating pedestal that supported the lens. Filled with carefully filtered kerosene brought daily to the tower from the oil storage house, the tank was pumped up by hand at intervals each night with enough air pressure to operate the light until dawn. The kerosene, vaporized by being passed over its own Bunsen flame, created a light dramatically more efficient and powerful than the old concentric wick lamp that burned the fuel directly. Ralph Tinkham identified a further key: the fragile, specially manufactured mantles that housed the flame

> *"We lived in the house nearest the tower. Dad could sit in his rocker and watch the light from his kitchen window. When the light revolved, it would flash on the fog-signal chimney. He could count the flashes for a minute or two and tell exactly if it was right on time. If it wasn't, he'd be up there in half a minute."*
>
> —CLARENCE H. YOUNG

and produced by incandescence "a pure white light so brilliant it can not be observed with the naked eye."

Split Rock keepers, while neglecting to wear the recommended dark goggles, nevertheless avoided the lantern deck while the lens was in motion so as not to confront the formidable eye of the beacon. Its glare—officially visible for 22 miles—was seen by fishermen as far away as Grand Marais, more than 60 miles distant. From April to December throughout nearly six decades, the beam flashed unfailingly at 10-second intervals across the busy shipping lanes of Lake Superior. When the light station and fog signal were electrified in 1940, the kerosene vapor lamp was finally retired and replaced by a 1,000-watt light bulb.

Keeper Covell with Split Rock's Fresnel lens, about 1930

Split Rock Lighthouse, *oil painting by Mike Lynch, 1988*

TONIC FOR A TARDY SIGNAL

THE DETERMINATION of Young and Covell to keep the light shining at all costs was on occasion put to severe test. The cable broke, the weights jammed in the center mast, the lamp fouled, the brass fuel tank leaked, or the leathers in the hand pump gave out. But the most strenuous labors occurred when the keepers themselves were pressed into duty as part of an emergency human backup system to keep the beacon in service. Two keepers spent the graveyard shift of more than one chilly night in the tower turning the lens by hand.

One such instance took place in April 1929. Discovering that the lens was running slow, Keeper Covell made an unsuccessful trip to Two Harbors to buy mercury for the bearing surface. That night he and a young assistant saw no choice but to stand in the watch room and turn the lens by hand, measuring its progress with a marine stopwatch in order to achieve the vital flash every 10 seconds that denoted Split

Rock. The following day they drained the mercury float and "washed" accumulated rust out of the existing mercury with kerosene. After the nearly 250 pounds of liquid were returned to the container, the lens turned faster, but for a second consecutive night the men were obliged to stand duty spinning the lens pedestal by hand.

On the third day the Two Harbors druggist arrived personally at the station to fill the keeper's unusual prescription: an eight-ounce medicine bottle holding eight pounds of mercury. This added dosage—minus a few tiny drops for Covell's daughter to play with—promptly restored the light to its normal rotation. Ironically, the cost of $3 per pound for the mercury outraged Covell's superiors in Detroit, and instead of being commended for his shrewd diagnosis and persistent efforts he was forced to account for the lavish expenditure by a further letter and a formal receipt from the druggist.

A SHOWPLACE
FOR VISITORS
~

SPLIT ROCK LIGHTHOUSE, as the name suggests, has had a divided personality. This fissure in its identity can perhaps be traced to a single event: the opening of the North Shore highway in 1924. What was once a forbidding fortress of rock and pine, accessible only by water, where lighthouse keepers stood a moonlight vigil in solitude and loneliness, became in a few short years an attraction so besieged with visitors that the keepers-turned-tour-guides often found themselves trapped in the crowded tower through lunch and even dinner.

Scarcely six weeks after the light was commissioned in 1910, Keeper Young briefly recorded in the lighthouse log: "A party of visitors from Split Rock." For the next decade and a half, traffic to the lighthouse included neighboring fishermen and an occasional wayward traveler. Local fisherman Edgar Lind claimed to have been the first to sign the now-lost visitors' register that remained in the fog signal building until 1936, when a heavy visitation in the month of July filled its last page.

A crude road connecting the new North Shore highway to the lighthouse reservation wound down to the boathouse in 1925. "First visitors over new road," read a matter-of-fact log entry in late April. On consecutive Sundays in June, Keeper Young recorded the then-remarkable totals of 27 and 15 visitors. The next summer a Duluth newspaper eulogized the attraction with the headline "Tourists Love the Place." The story prophesied exuberantly: "Tourists by the thousands will visit the great Split Rock light and its environment this year. They will be amazed to find this great ocean beacon in the center of North America. They will note with pleasure how carefully the American government safeguards its coasts for its mariners." What had once been the holiday preserve of local boating enthusiasts venturing out on the

> *"They keep a register on which historic names from far off places appear. They even, on occasion, dispense generous hospitality."*
>
> —*DULUTH HERALD,* 1926

The family of William Roleff, a Two Harbors photographer, camping at Silver Creek Cliff, 1922

half-dozen perfect Sundays in a summer had been opened up to the casual inspection of the world.

By the early 1930s about 5,000 people visited the light each year. Gradually the station developed a policy to handle this fundamental change in the way of life at Split Rock. Visiting hours were established so that the increased traffic would not interfere with station duties, since a keeper was required to escort all visitors. When scratches appeared on the lens, the sightseers were no longer permitted above the watch-room floor in the tower. At one time they had even enjoyed the luxury of dramatic open-air views from the lantern deck. The stepdaughter of First Assistant Luick remembered: "The wind is very powerful out there, and I have seen many tourists, mostly men, end up on their hands and knees crawling back to the door."

By 1935 the Lighthouse Service had come to recognize the station as "one of the 'show places' of the district." Nevertheless, when Keeper Covell pleaded for fences to ensure some privacy and protect his wife's flower garden, the service answered instead with permission to put up ineffectual warning signs. He was also reminded that it was his duty to escort personally as many of the visitors as possible while wearing a "clean

uniform." The following year, however, the service accepted his plan to erect a safety fence that still tops the wall at the base of the tower. The service also appointed an additional keeper for the summer months, "with the object of affording sufficient help at the station to permit the proper handling of visitors during the tourist season."

It was about time. Although his superiors in Detroit remained skeptical, Keeper Covell was not a man to speak without clear evidence: "The actual count taken from the visitors record book for the calendar year 1938 is 27,591. Registered for April and May, 123; June, 1,750; July, 8,533; August,

Awaiting the opening of the North Shore highway, 1924

The light station's truck, welcomed in 1934 by the keepers' children

A 1926 tourism brochure, with Split Rock Lighthouse a prominent attraction

10,820; September, 6,226; Oct., Nov., & Dec., 130. On several different times I made a count both by counting the people, then counting the registry, and found that less than one-third registered. So I estimated at least 100,000 visited the station during the season." This gave Split Rock a staggering five times as many visitors as any other station in the service.

When the Coast Guard absorbed the Lighthouse Service in 1939, it publicized Split Rock light as "probably the most visited lighthouse in the United States." The Civilian Conservation Corps built a new access road to the station in 1935, and in 1941 a gift shop sprang up at the entrance to the station. Although visits were curtailed during World War II, tourism rebounded rapidly at the war's close. In addition to the keepers, two young coast guardsmen were assigned to the station to act as summer guides, with living quarters established above the middle garage. When they were not available the tower remained closed, and no special effort was made to accommodate visitors.

Nevertheless, it was the tourist interest that kept the station operating long after the light and fog signal had been made obsolete by radar and other modern navigational equipment. Even after the light station was decommissioned and closed in 1969, visitors kept coming. This prompted the state of Minnesota to obtain the site from the Coast Guard and in 1971 open it to the public, but now as part of a new state park. Because of Split Rock's historical significance and the need to preserve its unique buildings, the Minnesota Historical Society began administering the light station as one of the state's historic sites.

Public interest in Split Rock continued to grow, and by the mid-1980s visitation to the lighthouse approached 200,000 annually, bringing to the manager and his family the same scrutiny felt by Keeper Covell's family more than a generation before. In 1986 the Split Rock Lighthouse History Center was opened to help interpret the story of the light station, its keepers, and their role in Great Lakes shipping. The state built campgrounds

"There are thousands of pictures taken of the station and shore line every month by tourists, press agents, and newsreel men. There is every kind of camera used from motion picture to pocket kodak."

—KEEPER COVELL, 1941

Tourists in front of the keepers' houses, about 1945

A coast guardsman oiling the clockwork mechanism that rotates the light's lens, about 1945

in the adjoining state park near the old fishing village at Little Two Harbors and developed a trail system to the lighthouse. The tower has been restored to the way it looked in 1920 under Keeper Pete Young.

Today, visitors to the site can enjoy a movie recounting the early days at Split Rock, view exhibits, and shop in the museum store. They can tour the fog signal building and the restored keeper's home and climb to the top of the lighthouse. Or they can sit at its base, 130 feet above the largest lake in the world, and sense the presence of the men and women who made Split Rock light station their home while making the waters of Lake Superior safer for the mariners who passed beneath the distinguished beacon.

From the air, a tidy site surrounded by second-growth forest, 1959

Tourists hiking in the state park

FACTS ABOUT SPLIT ROCK LIGHTHOUSE ∼

LIGHT STATION

Years of operation: 1910–69
Cost: $75,000 (land and buildings)
Administered by: U.S. Lighthouse Service, 1910–39
U.S. Coast Guard, 1939–69
Lake Superior elevation: 602 feet above sea level
Cliff height: 130 feet
Tower height: 54 feet
Light source: Incandescent oil-vapor (kerosene) lamp, 1910–39
1,000-watt electric bulb, 1940–69
Lens: 3rd-order bivalve Fresnel lens, manufactured by Barbier, Bernard and Turenne
Company, Paris, France
Official range: 22 miles
Flashing sequence: Once every 10 seconds (0.5-second flash every 9.5 seconds)

FOG SIGNAL

Years of operation: 1910–61
Powered by: Franklin 30-hp. gasoline-driven air compressors, manufactured by
Chicago Pneumatic Tool Company, 1910–31
Diesel compressors, 1932–61
Tone: Siren-blast, 1910–35
Type F diaphone ("be-you" sound), 1936–61
Sounding sequence: 2-second blast, 18-second silence
Effective range: 5 miles

Split Rock Lighthouse is now owned by the State of Minnesota and has been administered by the Minnesota Historical Society since 1976. Split Rock Lighthouse was placed on the National Register of Historic Places in 1969.

Lightning strike near Split Rock, about 1911